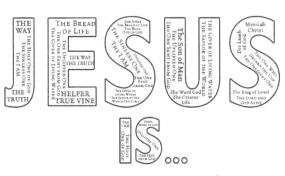

42 Days with Jesus from the Gospel of John

KEN BURTON

Foreword by Clarence DeLoach

XULON PRESS

Xulon Press
2301 Lucien Way #415
Maitland, FL 32751
407.339.4217
www.xulonpress.com

© 2021 by Ken Burton

All rights reserved solely by the author. The author guarantees all contents are original and do not infringe upon the legal rights of any other person or work. No part of this book may be reproduced in any form without the permission of the author. The views expressed in this book are not necessarily those of the publisher.

Unless otherwise indicated, Scripture quotations taken from the English Standard Version (ESV). Copyright © 2001 by Crossway, a publishing ministry of Good News Publishers. Used by permission. All rights reserved.

Printed in the United States of America.

ISBN-13: 978-1-6628-1348-1

TABLE OF CONTENTS

ABOUT THE AUTHOR xi
FOREWORD xiii
PREFACE xv
DEDICATION xvii

JESUS IS …

Lesson 1: **JESUS IS … THE WORD** *(JOHN 1:1–4, 14)* 1
Lesson 2: **JESUS IS … GOD** *(JOHN 1:1)* 3
Lesson 3: **JESUS IS … THE CREATOR** *(JOHN 1:3)* 5
Lesson 4: **JESUS IS … LIFE** *(JOHN 1:4; 5:25, 26; 10:10; 14:6; 20:30–31)* 7
Lesson 5: **JESUS IS …THE LIGHT** *(JOHN 1:4, 5; 3:19–21; 8:12; 9:5; 12:35–36)* 9
Lesson 6: **JESUS IS …THE SON** *(JOHN 1:14, 34, 39; 5:25; 11:27)* 11
Lesson 7: **JESUS IS … THE ONE WHO IS FULL OF GRACE AND TRUTH** *(John 1:14–17)* 13
Lesson 8: **JESUS IS … THE REVEALER OF THE FATHER** *(John 1:18)*. 15
Lesson 9: **JESUS IS … THE ONE WHO COMES AFTER BUT WHO WAS BEFORE** *(John 1:27, 30)* 17
Lesson 10: **JESUS IS … THE LAMB OF GOD** *(John 1:29, 36)*. 19

Lesson 11: **JESUS IS … THE MESSIAH/CHRIST**
(JOHN 1:41; 4:25–26; 11:27; 20:30–31) 21

Lesson 12: **JESUS IS … THE FULFILLMENT OF MOSES AND THE PROPHETS** *(John 1:45; 5:39, 45–47; 12:14, 15; 19:24, 28, 36–37)* 23

Lesson 13: **JESUS IS … THE KING OF ISRAEL**
(John 1:49; 12:15; 18:33–38) 25

Lesson 14: **JESUS IS … THE SON OF MAN**
(John 1:51) 27

Lesson 15: **JESUS IS … THE TEACHER COME FROM GOD**
(John 3:2; 11:28; 20:16) 29

Lesson 16: **JESUS IS … THE UPLIFTED ONE** *(John 3:14; 8:28; 12:32–33; 19:18–30)* 31

Lesson 17: **JESUS IS … THE ONE SENT FROM GOD**
(John 3:34; 4:34; 5:30, 37–38; 6:38–39, 44, 57; 7:16, 18, 28–29, 33; 8:16, 18, 26, 29, 42; 9:4; 10:36; 11:42; 12:44–46; 14:24; 15:21; 17:8, 18, 21, 23, 25; 20:21) 35

Lesson 18: **JESUS IS … THE GIVER OF LIVING WATER**
(John 4:10–14; 7:37–39) 37

Lesson 19: **JESUS IS … THE SAVIOR OF THE WORLD**
(John 4:42) 39

Lesson 20: **JESUS IS … THE JUDGE** *(John 5:19–30; 12:48)* 41

Lesson 21: **JESUS IS … THE BREAD OF LIFE** *(John 6:35, 41, 48, 51)* 43

Lesson 22: **JESUS IS … THE HOLY ONE OF GOD**
(John 6:69) 45

Lesson 23: **JESUS IS … THE ONE WHO SPOKE LIKE NO ONE ELSE** *(John 7:46)* 47

Lesson 24: **JESUS IS … THE SINLESS ONE** *(John 8:46)* ... 49

Lesson 25: **JESUS IS … THE I AM** *(John 8:58)* 53

Lesson 26: **JESUS IS ... THE DOOR OF THE SHEEPFOLD** *(John 10:1–10)*.................. 55

Lesson 27: **JESUS IS ... THE GOOD SHEPHERD** *(John 10:11–30)* 57

Lesson 28: **JESUS IS ... THE RESURRECTION AND THE LIFE** *(JOHN 11:25)* 59

Lesson 29: **JESUS IS ... THE ONE WHO GLORIFIES THE FATHER** *(John 12:23, 28; 13:1; 17:1–5)* 61

Lesson 30: **JESUS IS ... THE HUMBLE SERVANT** *(JOHN 13:1–20)*................................ 63

Lesson 31: **JESUS IS ... COMING AGAIN** *(JOHN 14:1–4)*.................................. 65

Lesson 32: **JESUS IS ... THE WAY** *(JOHN 14:6)* 67

Lesson 33: **JESUS IS ... THE TRUTH** *(JOHN 14:6)* 69

Lesson 34: **JESUS IS ... THE ONE WHO SENDS THE HELPER** *(JOHN 14:16–18, 26; 15:26–27; 16:7–15)*...71

Lesson 35: **JESUS IS ... THE TRUE VINE** *(JOHN 15:1–11)*................................. 73

Lesson 36: **JESUS IS ... THE ONE WHO LAYS DOWN HIS LIFE FOR HIS FRIENDS** *(JOHN 15:13–14)*.......... 75

Lesson 37: **JESUS IS ... THE GREATEST EXAMPLE OF LOVE** *(JOHN 15:12)* 77

Lesson 38: **JESUS IS ... THE ONE WHO OVERCOMES THE WORLD** *(JOHN 16:33)*..................... 79

Lesson 39: **JESUS IS ... THE ONE WHO DRINKS THE CUP** *(JOHN 18:11)*................................. 81

Lesson 40: **JESUS IS ... THE OBEDIENT ONE** *(JOHN 17:4; 19:30)* 83

Lesson 41: **JESUS IS ... LORD AND GOD** *(JOHN 20:28)*................................. 85

Lesson 42: **JESUS IS ... ALIVE** *(John 20:1–21:25)* 87

ABOUT THE AUTHOR

Ken Burton was raised in Parkersburg, WV. He married the former Diane Petty, August 2, 1975. He graduated from Parkersburg High School in 1971. He then received an A.A. degree from Ohio Valley College in 1973 and completed a B.A. degree in Bible from Harding University in 1975. He completed work on an M.A. degree from Alabama Christian School of Religion (now Amridge University), Montgomery, Alabama in 1984 and continued with post-Masters work at Amridge University from 2007–2015.

Ken has preached for the following congregations among churches of Christ: Cairo, WV; Eight Mile Ridge, Reader, WV; Hillview Terrace, Moundsville, WV; South Thornton Street, Piggott, AR; Willow Avenue, Cookeville, TN. He has been preaching for the College and North church of Christ in Mountain Home, AR since August of 2003.

Ken has been privileged to participate in mission trips to Italy (1971–72); Guyana and Suriname, South America (1987–90, and 1992); and India (1996, 1999, 2003, and 2005).

FOREWORD

It is a joy to commend to you this short volume, *Jesus Is—42 Days with Jesus from the Gospel of John*, written by my friend and brother, Ken Burton. I have known Ken and his family for more than fifty years. He was a teenager when I first met him when I preached in the Ohio Valley. It became evident to me early on that Ken had the potential to become an effective preacher in our great brotherhood. Indeed, he has done that.

He is one of the most diligent and conscientious students of the Word that I have known. By training and experience he has done a great work in teaching, preaching, and radio evangelism wherever he has been located.

There is no question in my mind that the greatest of questions is, "Who is Jesus?" If we don't get that answer right, we will never know God or understand the Bible. He reveals the Father, for Jesus said, "He who has seen me has seen the Father" *(John 14:9)*. Further, He is the key that unlocks the Bible to our minds with more than three hundred references to Him in the Old Testament. He is the living Word that reveals the written Word.

Never in our lifetime has there been more confusion about who Jesus is than today. The Gospel of John has the clearest purpose statement in the Bible, "… but these are written that you may believe that Jesus is the Christ, the Son of God, and that believing you may have life in His name" *(John 20:31)*. The key verb in John is "believe" which requires both knowledge and volition. The result of such knowledge and volition is obedience.

Brother Burton has given us forty-two portraits of Jesus with a brief study of those descriptions in context and then at the end he has given added Scriptures that relate to the theme. These could be used for personal devotions in the family. They could be used for Bible class material. Men who extend the Lord's invitation will find these materials helpful. These studies will enable them to answer and defend the truth about Jesus when confronted by religious cults and liberal theology.

We are indebted to the author who sends forth this volume for the glory of God and the edification of His servants.

Clarence DeLoach
Cookeville, TN
February 25, 2021

PREFACE

The Gospel of John has been the starting point for many Bible students. John's presentation of Jesus is both simple and profound. This book is written for anyone who is searching for a deeper understanding of who Jesus is, what Jesus did, and what Jesus is still doing. By working through this book, one will study through the whole Gospel of John.

The book can be used in the following ways:
1) As a six-week daily devotional. While each lesson is brief, enough Scripture references are included to provide material for in-depth study.
2) As a guide for family devotionals. Parents will be able to adapt the chapters to the ages of their children, providing them with a good foundation on the Life of Jesus as presented by the Beloved Disciple.
3) For small-group studies. The Scripture references included in the "For Further Reading" sections will encourage discussion and can lead to discovering a larger number of relevant cross-references.
4) For Bible classes for teens through adults. Experienced teachers will be able to teach one lesson per chapter, while others might be more comfortable combining a couple of chapters per lesson.

I am grateful to my friend and mentor, Clarence DeLoach, for writing the Foreword to this book. He has impacted my life in more ways than I can tell, both as a preacher and as a friend. He and his family are deeply loved by my family.

I am also grateful to Pat Coomer, with whom I worked for several years at the Willow Avenue church of Christ in Cookeville, Tennessee, where I preached and she was the secretary. She read the manuscript carefully and found several errors I was able to correct before the book was published. Any errors that remain are my own!

In nearly fifty years of preaching, I have consulted numerous sources on the Gospel of John. Those I have consulted most frequently are the commentaries by Guy N. Woods, Leon Morris, F. F. Bruce, William Hendriksen, and William Barclay. Dr. Morris wrote several additional monographs on the Gospel of John, and Professor Bruce wrote extensively on the life of Jesus, and those works have also been both enlightening and useful.

My prayer is that this book will be used for the glory of God and for building up His people!

DEDICATION

To my wife, Diane, without whose encouragement this book would have been neither attempted nor finished.

Lesson 1
JESUS IS ... THE WORD
(JOHN 1:1–4, 14)

John begins his account of the life of Jesus with a reference to eternity past. *"In the beginning"* takes us to the first verse of the first book of the Bible. In fact, what John says about Jesus in these verses is exactly what we read in Genesis 1:1: *"In the beginning God created the heavens and the earth."* Concerning Jesus, John states, *"All things were made through him, and without him was not anything made that was made."* In Genesis 1, the writer says, *"And God said... and it was so."* His powerful word brought all things into existence. John identifies the powerful word of God as Jesus. Before he became flesh and was given the name "Jesus," he was known as the eternal Word of God.

We know this "Word" John introduces to us is Jesus, because in John 1:14 he states, *"The Word became flesh and dwelt among us, and we have seen his glory, glory as of the only Son from the Father, full of grace and truth."*

When we think of a "word," communication is the first thing that comes to mind. Although John probably had more than that in mind when he used this term, communication is what Jesus is all about. God communicates to us most clearly through His Son Jesus Christ *(Hebrews 1:1–4)*. Not only do the words Jesus spoke, the example he set for us, and the miracles he did communicate to us, but especially his death on the cross communicates God's never-ending, never-failing love toward us *(John 3:16)*.

If you desire to hear what God has to say to you, pay close attention to Jesus. He is God's greatest communication of Himself to us!

FOR FURTHER READING: John 1:1–18; Genesis 1:1–2:3; Philippians 2:5–11; Colossians 1:15–20; Hebrews 1:1–4.

NOTES

Lesson 2

JESUS IS ... GOD
(JOHN 1:1)

Of all the descriptions of Jesus presented in the New Testament, this is the most remarkable, and the most objectionable. While many are quite willing to accept Jesus as a great teacher, the best man who ever lived, and perhaps even a worker of miracles, they will balk at acknowledging Jesus as "God."

One reason for this hesitancy is that the word "God" is normally used to refer to "the Father," and we know Jesus is not "the Father." However, the word "God" also refers to the quality of deity, to one who shares the characteristics that distinguish God from humans. This leads to the further inquiry into the nature of the Godhead, or "trinity." This is also a stumbling-block to many who approach everything—including Scripture—with a mathematical, analytical precision.

The statement of John, right here at the beginning of his Gospel, that "the Word was God," intentionally sets the stage for all that John will record in the rest of the book. Attempts to translate the verse differently, such as "God was the Word," or "the Word was a god," create more problems than they propose to solve.

Jesus is not "just" a man, not even "just" the best and greatest man who ever lived. As C. S. Lewis (and others) have clearly demonstrated, if Jesus were not what He claimed to be, He was not a good man at all!

Later in John's book, he quotes Jesus as saying, "Truly, truly, I say to you, before Abraham was, I am" *(John 8:58)*, "I and the Father are One" *(John 10:30)*, and "He who has seen me has seen the Father" *(John 14:9)*. These claims, and others like them, were understood even by Jesus' enemies to be claims to equality with the Father, and (in their eyes) blasphemy.

If Jesus' claims were false, he would have been "guilty as charged." But because his claims were vindicated, Jesus is thus "Lord and God" *(John 20:28)*.

FOR FURTHER READING: Philippians 2:5–11; Colossians 1:15–20; Hebrews 1:1–4; Titus 2:11–14; 2 Peter 1:1, 2; Revelation 5:1–14.

NOTES

Lesson 3

JESUS IS ... THE CREATOR
(JOHN 1:3)

"**A**ll things were made through Him" sounds like a reference to God, the Father, doesn't it? But in this context this statement is made concerning the Word who "became flesh and dwelt among us" *(John 1:14)*.

Genesis 1 supplies a "hint" that all three persons of the Godhead took part in the creation: "God created" *(Genesis 1:1)*, "the Spirit of God was hovering over the face of the waters" *(Genesis 1:2)*, and "Let us make man in our image, after our likeness" *(Genesis 1:26)*. Only with the further revelation of Scripture does this become clearer.

When writers of the Bible extol God's power, they often praise Him for His creation *(cf. Exodus 20:11; 2 Kings 19:15; 1 Chronicles 16:23–27 [Psalm 96:1–6]; Nehemiah 9:6; Psalm 146:5–7; Isaiah 45:18; Acts 14:15; Romans 1:20)*. The power to speak and bring everything that is "visible and invisible" into being is power beyond human comprehension. When this power is attributed to the One Whose first resting place was a feeding trough, Who was known in Nazareth as the carpenter's son, Who traveled throughout Galilee and Judea preaching and teaching without a place to rest His head, and Who ultimately was nailed to a cross, the ability to comprehend becomes even harder, doesn't it? But when we accept John's statement as true, the miracles and resurrection of Jesus are less incredible, aren't they?

When we realize what John has done in these first few verses, it is mind-boggling! He has asserted that the man Jesus existed from all eternity, shared all the qualities of deity, and was the agent by Whom everything in the universe came into being! As was noted in yesterday's reading, the option of accepting Jesus as a good man without acknowledging His unique nature in relation to both God and humans is not available!

FOR FURTHER READING: Proverbs 8:12–36; 1 Corinthians 1:18–31; Colossians 1:15–20; Hebrews 1:1–4; Revelation 3:14.

NOTES

Lesson 4

JESUS IS ... LIFE
(JOHN 1:4; 5:25, 26; 10:10; 14:6; 20:30–31)

When John wrote *"in Him was Life" (John 1:4)*, he put his readers on notice that the account of Jesus that follows is more than the biography of a good, or even of a great, man. He wants us to understand that the man about whom he wrote is vital to our existence. Already he has said that we were made through Him, indicating that the physical existence we experience is dependent upon Jesus. But John means more than that. This introduction to the theme of "life" is expanded in the other passages listed above.

For example, in John 5:25, 26, Jesus stated, *"Truly, truly, I say to you, an hour is coming, and is now here, when the dead will hear the voice of the Son of God, and those who hear will live. For as the Father has life in himself, so he has granted the Son also to have life in himself."* "Life" in the Gospel of John means more than day-to-day existence. It means more than the number of years one lives on this earth. It means more than the legacy one leaves behind when this "life" comes to its end. "Life" in the sense John uses it has to do with life that doesn't end when physical death occurs. It refers not just to the immortality of the soul, but also to the resurrection of the body after physical death.

In John 10:10, Jesus makes it even more clear that this is what He came to provide: *"The thief comes only to steal and kill and destroy. I came that they may have life and have it abundantly."* The "abundant life" consists in something other than material wealth, fame, glory, and power. One may accumulate all these markers of "success," and live a bankrupt life *(cf. Luke 12:13–21).*

In John 14:6, Jesus explains to his disciples, *"I am ... the life."* In other words, there is no real life without Jesus. One may exist on this planet for an above-average lifespan and still miss "life." Note that Jesus is not "*a* life;" He is "***the* life!**"

While the first 18 verses of John's Gospel provide an introduction to the themes he develops in the body of his writing, the purpose for which he wrote is stated near the end of the Gospel, in John 20:30, 31, where he wrote, *"Now Jesus did many other signs in the presence of the disciples, which are not written in this book; but these are written so that you may believe that Jesus is the Christ, the Son of God, and that by believing you may have life in his name."*

FOR FURTHER READING: John 3:14–17; 1 Timothy 6:11–16; Titus 1:1–4; 1 John 5:6–12; Revelation 1:17–18.

NOTES

Lesson 5

JESUS IS ...THE LIGHT
(JOHN 1:4, 5; 3:19–21; 8:12; 9:5; 12:35–36)

"Light" is a word that needs no definition, at least not as far as our experience is concerned. We know when it is light, and we know when it is dark. There is a time and a place for darkness, but most of us would prefer not to live in perpetual darkness.

But when John wrote of Jesus in John 1:4, 5, *"In Him was life, and the life was the light of men. The light shines in the darkness, and the darkness has not overcome it,"* he is using the word "light" as a metaphor for Jesus as the One who exposes sin for what it truly is, and sinners for what they truly are! This becomes clear when the other Scriptures are read and studied.

In John 3:19–21 Jesus states, *"And this is the judgment: the light has come into the world, and people loved the darkness rather than the light because their works were evil. For everyone who does wicked things hates the light and does not come to the light, lest his works should be exposed. But whoever does what is true comes to the light, so that it may be clearly seen that his works have been carried out in God."* Jesus is the One who is rejected when one chooses to love his or her sinful lifestyle rather than to conform to Jesus' standard.

In John 8:12 and 9:5, Jesus uses the metaphor of Himself when He says, *"I am the light of the world,"* and *"As long as I am in the world, I am the light of the world."*

His standard of perfection stands in stark contrast to the sinfulness of humanity.

John 12:35, 36 comes near the end of John's record of Jesus' public ministry. John 13–17 record Jesus' intimate conversation with and prayer for His disciples, and John 18–21 tell of Jesus' arrest, trial, crucifixion, resurrection, and appearances to the disciples. So, near the end of Jesus' public life, He challenges the people (and us!) by saying, *"The light is among you for a little while longer. Walk while you have the light, lest darkness overtake you. The one who walks in the darkness does not know where he is going. While you have the light, believe in the light, that you may become sons of light."*

Are you a "son [child] of light"?

FOR FURTHER READING: 2 Corinthians 4:1–6; Ephesians 4:17–24; 5:7–14; Colossians 1:9–14; 1 Thessalonians 5:1–11; 1 John 1:5–10; 2:7–11.

NOTES

Lesson 6

JESUS IS ...THE SON
(JOHN 1:14, 34, 39; 5:25; 11:27)

There is a problem when Jesus is presented as the "Son." In our experience, a son is always younger than his father (and a daughter is younger than her mother)! But John has already stated that Jesus, as the Word, shares eternity with God, His Father. Thus, He is not "younger" than the Father! How can Jesus be the "Son of God"?

When we realize that the Semitic expression *"Son of ..."* was the usual way of expressing likeness or exhibiting the characteristics of the quality described, then it helps us to understand what John and the rest of the writers of the New Testament meant when they used that expression *(cf. Acts 4:36)*. As "Son of God," Jesus perfectly represents the Father to the world and demonstrated all the qualities of God in human form. As "Son of Man," He is the perfect Man, and is thus qualified to be our atoning sacrifice.

In John 1:14, we read, *"And the Word became flesh and dwelt among us, and we have seen his glory, glory as of the only Son from the Father, full of grace and truth."*

In John 1:32–34, John the Baptizer states, *"I saw the Spirit descend from heaven like a dove, and it remained on him. I myself did not know him, but he who sent me to baptize with water said to me, 'He on whom you see the Spirit descend and remain, this is he who baptizes with the Holy Spirit.' And I have seen and have borne witness that this is the Son of God."*

Jesus, in John 5:25–27, boldly states, *"Truly, truly, I say to you, an hour is coming, and is now here, when the dead will hear the voice of the Son of God, and those who hear will live. For as the Father has life in himself, so he has granted the Son also to have life in himself. And he has given him authority to execute judgment, because he is the Son of Man."*

Martha, the sister of Lazarus, made a remarkable confession in John 11:27 when she said to Jesus, *"Yes, Lord; I believe that you are the Christ, the Son of God, who is coming into the world."*

FOR FURTHER READING: Romans 1:1–7; 8:12–17; Galatians 4:1–7; Hebrews 1:1–14.

NOTES

Lesson 7

JESUS IS ... THE ONE WHO IS FULL OF GRACE AND TRUTH
(John 1:14–17)

When John wrote this description of Jesus in this text, he was reflecting on the entire life and ministry of Jesus, including His death, resurrection, and ascension. As a "point of departure" for the account of Jesus' life that follows, this summary sets the stage for the reader to be looking for the various ways Jesus fulfills this statement.

When Jesus interacts with Nicodemus in John 3, we see Jesus speaking truth to one who could easily have been hostile to hearing it.

When Jesus converses with the Samaritan woman in John 4, He demonstrates both grace and truth: *grace* because it was unconventional for Him to talk to a woman, especially a foreign woman with a sordid past, and then to agree to stay another two days in their town; *truth* because He shows her his ability to "tell all she has ever done" and refutes both the Samaritan and Jewish belief in the proper place to worship God.

When Jesus is confronted by His opponents in John 5, He demonstrates grace by telling them the truth, and points them to the "witnesses" that should convince them of His identity *(John 5:30–47)*.

In fact, this may be precisely what John is wanting us to see: God's grace is extended to us by means of making the truth available to us. Rather than seeing grace and truth as at odds with each other, which is the perspective of our modern culture, Scripture is God's truth revealing His grace. And as the living Word, Jesus embodies both grace and truth.

For Further Reading: As you read the Gospel of John, look for the ways Jesus reveals God's grace and God's truth in the situations John describes. The same approach can be used as you read Matthew, Mark, and Luke as well.

NOTES

Lesson 8

JESUS IS ... THE REVEALER OF THE FATHER
(JOHN 1:18)

Building on the imagery of John 1:1–4, John presents Jesus as the One Who is in the unique position to fully reveal God's character to humans as a human. It is one thing to read about God in Scripture, and to be made aware of His power, His love, His holiness, His knowledge, and all His other "attributes." But to see God as a human being, demonstrating God's power, love, holiness, knowledge, and all the other attributes, makes God more real for us.

That is precisely what Jesus has done for us. Rather than having to rely on the narratives and prophecies of the Old Testament for our knowledge of God, we have the great privilege of looking at the life, words, character, and works of Jesus. In Him we can see just what God is like.

Josh McDowell, in his classic work *Evidence that Demands a Verdict*, included a section "If God Became Man," in which he presents the kind of man we should expect if God should choose to become a man. Jesus is that man! He fulfills every expectation of what God would be like in a human body. Jesus' dealings with His opponents is in line with God's dealings with His rebellious people in the Old Testament. Jesus' tenderness and compassion precisely parallels God's compassion toward His wayward people. Jesus' selfless love is the exact representation of God's inexhaustible love toward His people.

In every way, Jesus perfectly reveals the Father in heaven!

FOR FURTHER READING: John 10:30; 14:8–11; the whole book of Hosea.

NOTES

Lesson 9

JESUS IS ... THE ONE WHO COMES AFTER BUT WHO WAS BEFORE
(JOHN 1:27, 30)

John the Baptizer was born six months before Jesus, according to Luke's account *(Luke 1:24–26)*. But when he is asked about Jesus, he seems to have his chronology backwards. He tells the representatives from Jerusalem that there is One coming after Him who has greater authority *(John 1:27)*. Later, he refers to Jesus again and states, "This is he of whom I said, 'After me comes a man who ranks before me, because he was before me' " *(John 1:30)*.

Can you imagine the perplexity of John's audience when they heard these words? How can one who is younger exist before the older one? This "riddle" is similar to one we read in Matthew 22:41–46, where Jesus asked, *"If David calls [the Messiah] Lord, how can he be his son?"* The question is based on David's statement in Psalm 110:1. The ancestor, especially one as great as David, should have greater honor than his descendant. And yet David refers to his descendant as "Lord." The same chronological puzzle exists there as in John 1:27, 30.

We have the answer in the earlier part of John 1. When John (the apostle and author of the fourth Gospel, not John the Baptizer whose statements are recorded in the texts we are considering) states concerning the Word that He was in the beginning, that He was with God, and that He was God, the answer becomes clear. John the Baptizer, who pointed his audience to Jesus, recognized that Jesus not only ranked ahead of him, but existed before him, even though He was born six months later!

FOR FURTHER READING: Luke 1:5–45; Psalm 110:1–7; Matthew 22:15–46.

NOTES

Lesson 10
JESUS IS ... THE LAMB OF GOD
(JOHN 1:29, 36)

What picture comes to mind when you think of a lamb? I think of an animal that is gentle and relatively harmless, skittish around humans, and cuddly in appearance.

> The picture that would have come to the minds of John's audience would have been similar, but with more depth. Given their background with Jewish ceremony, the lamb imagery would have had greater significance.
>
> A lamb was sacrificed every morning and every evening as a burnt offering *(Exodus 29:38–46)*.
>
> A lamb was sacrificed to redeem the firstborn of an "unclean" animal, such as a donkey *(Exodus 13:13)*.
>
> A lamb was offered to redeem the firstborn son in each family *(Exodus 13:11–16)*.
>
> A lamb could be offered as a peace offering *(Leviticus 3:1–10, esp. v. 7)*.
>
> A lamb could be offered as a sin offering *(Leviticus 5:27–5:6)*.
>
> But the lamb was especially associated with the Passover feast *(Exodus 12; 1 Corinthians 5:7)*.

John's audience would have had all these images in mind when they heard him say concerning Jesus, *"Behold, the Lamb of God that takes away the sin of the world!"* Sacrifice for sin, for redemption, and for establishing peace with God—Jesus accomplished it all as "the Lamb of God"!

Have you been washed in the blood of the Lamb of God?

FOR FURTHER READING: In addition to the passages listed above, see also Acts 20:28; Ephesians 1:3–10; 2 Corinthians 5:21; Colossians 1:15–23; 1 Peter 1:13–21.

NOTES

Lesson 11

JESUS IS ... THE MESSIAH/CHRIST
(JOHN 1:41; 4:25–26; 11:27; 20:30–31)

We are so accustomed to hearing the expression "Jesus Christ" as a proper name that we have lost the excitement that must have filled the hearts of those who first recognized in Jesus the fulfillment of their longings, hopes, yearnings, and expectations. "Jesus" was the name given at His birth *(cf. Matthew 1:18–25)*. "Christ," rather than being His surname, is a title. From the Hebrew/Aramaic languages the word is translated "Messiah." From Greek it is translated (or transliterated) "Christ." The title refers to one who had been anointed to fill a role. Kings were anointed as a sign of their designation to the office (*1 Samuel 10:1; 16:1–13; 1 Kings 19:15–18)*. Priests were anointed before they assumed the responsibilities of their office *(Leviticus 8:22–30)*. Prophets were sometimes anointed as well *(1 Kings 19:16)*.

The Old Testament prophets had foretold the coming of One Who would be a Messiah/Christ without parallel. While the kings and priests of the Old Testament were "messiahs" in the sense of their anointing and filling the roles of the office assigned them, they were mere shadows of a greater Messiah to come. This expectation was based on such passages as 2 Samuel 7:1–17; Psalm 110; Isaiah 9:6–8; Ezekiel 34:20–24; 37:24–28. There had been a period of nearly four hundred years since any prophet from God had appeared among the people, when suddenly John the Baptizer began proclaiming his message, calling the people to believe on the One coming after him. Many wondered if John were himself the Messiah/Christ *(John 1:19–28)*.

When Andrew announced, "We have found the Messiah," the announcement would have been like a thunderbolt to Peter. Andrew's excitement must have been contagious, for Peter immediately went with his brother to meet this Jesus of whom Andrew was speaking.

As startling as the announcement was to Peter, even more startling was Peter's announcement to a large crowd of Jews and proselytes in Acts 2:36, when he proclaimed, *"Let all the house of Israel therefore know for certain that God has made him both Lord and Christ, this Jesus whom you crucified."*

FOR FURTHER READING: When reading your New Testament, try substituting the word "Messiah" or "King" for the word "Christ" when it is used in connection with the name of Jesus. It may help you to remember to think of Jesus' roles as Prophet, Priest, and King.

NOTES

LESSON 12

JESUS IS ... THE FULFILLMENT OF MOSES AND THE PROPHETS
(JOHN 1:45; 5:39, 45–47; 12:14, 15; 19:24, 28, 36–37)

Just as startling as Andrew's announcement, *"We have found the Messiah"* was Philip's statement to Nathanael, *"We have found Him of whom Moses in the Law and also the prophets wrote, Jesus of Nazareth, the son of Joseph."* From an unremarkable town in Galilee, born into an unremarkable family, comes One Who is supposed to fulfill all the prophecies in the Old Testament writings! This seemed absurd to Nathanael *(see John 1:46)* and seemed absurd to many others as well (note the opposition Jesus aroused among the Pharisees and Sadducees).

But when His life is examined, it is clear that Jesus did indeed fulfill all the things written concerning the Coming One. In John 5:39–47, Jesus sets forth this same line of reasoning, pleading with His opponents to search their Scriptures and find the true life God was offering them through Jesus. He appeals to the prophets and to Moses as witnesses to the claims He made. The prophecies are Jesus' "fingerprints" or "DNA," identifying Him as the One through Whom the Father would save the world.

To mention only a few of the many ways Moses wrote of Jesus *(John 5:46)*, in Genesis Jesus is the seed of the woman *(Genesis 3:15)*, the seed of Abraham *(Genesis 12:1–3; Galatians 3:16)*, and the scepter from Judah *(Genesis 49:10;*

Revelation 5:5). In Exodus, Jesus is the Passover Lamb *(Exodus 12)*, the bread from heaven *(Exodus 16:4ff.; John 6)*, and the rock *(Exodus 17:1–6; 1 Corinthians 10:1–4)*. In Leviticus He is foreshadowed by the priesthood *(cf. Hebrews 7)* and the sacrifices *(cf. Hebrews 9, 10)*. In Numbers He is the serpent lifted up for the salvation of the people *(Numbers 21:4–9; John 3:14, 15)*. In Deuteronomy He is the One Who is cursed by being hanged on the tree (*Deuteronomy 21:23; Galatians 3: 13) and the prophet like Moses (Deuteronomy 18:15-19; Acts 3:22, 23; John 1: 21; 6:14; 7:40)*.

FOR FURTHER READING: Psalm 22; Isaiah 53; Luke 24:13–27, 44–49.

NOTES

Lesson 13

JESUS ... THE KING OF ISRAEL
(John 1:49; 12:15; 18:33–38)

One of the roles the promised Messiah would fill would be "king," or ruler over God's people. Since the time of David, the people of Israel had anticipated a great king to come from David's lineage. This was based on the promise and covenant God made with David recorded in 2 Samuel 7:1–17 and 1 Chronicles 17:1–15.

David was a powerful figure in the history of Israel. He is known to us as the one who killed Goliath, the Philistine giant *(1 Samuel 17)*, the shepherd who became king *(1 Samuel 16:1–13)*, the mighty warrior through whom God gave Israel victory over the surrounding nations *(2 Samuel 7:1; 1 Chronicles 18:1–17)*, as a writer of nearly half of the Psalms, and as "a man after God's own heart" *(1 Samuel 13:14)*. It was natural that the people of Jesus' day were expecting a figure who would accomplish many of the things David had achieved, especially defeating Israel's enemies, especially Rome.

By reading the Gospels one can immediately see that Jesus was different from David. Jesus did not have a throne in Jerusalem, and He did not fight battles with military strategy and deadly weapons. In what sense, then, did Jesus fill the role of Israel's king? Nathanael recognized Jesus as "the king of Israel" *(John 1:49)*, and John quotes a prophecy from Zechariah 9:9 as Jesus entered Jerusalem publicly a few days before His death that states, *"Fear not, daughter of Zion; behold, your king is coming, sitting on a donkey's colt!"* *(John 12:15)*. When Jesus was crucified Pilate had written the charge against Him in these words: *"Jesus of Nazareth, the King of the Jews" (John 19:19–22).*

In what sense is Jesus king? John 18:36 helps us to understand this important question. Jesus, in his conversation with Pilate, declares, *"My kingdom is not of this world. If my kingdom were of this world, my servants would have been fighting, that I might not be delivered over to the Jews. But my kingdom is not from the world."*

The Jews of Jesus' day were expecting a kingdom "of this world" that would resemble David's glorious kingdom from the distant past. Many people today are still looking for Jesus to return and establish that kind of a kingdom. But Jesus plainly states that His kingdom is not a materialistic, earthly, worldly, physical kingdom. His kingdom was established in the days of the apostles *(Matthew 16:18–19; Colossians 1:13; Revelation 1:9)*. It is a spiritual kingdom, established on spiritual values, changing men and women, not by force of physical weapons, but by changing their minds through the power of the Gospel *(cf. 2 Corinthians 10:3–6; Ephesians 6:10–20; Romans 1:14–17)*!

FOR FURTHER READING: Isaiah 9:6–7; Matthew 1:1; Luke 1:26–38; Galatians 6:16.

NOTES

Lesson 14
JESUS IS ... THE SON OF MAN
(John 1:51)

The phrase "Son of Man" is found thirteen times in the Gospel of John *(John 1:51; 3:13, 14; 5:27; 6:27, 53, 62; 8:28; 9:35; 12:23, 34; 13:31)*. In eleven of those cases it is used by Jesus to refer to Himself. The two times it is used by others *(John 12:34)* it is in a question from the crowd in response to something Jesus had said about "the Son of Man." It is His favorite self-description. Jesus uses the phrase "Son of Man" twenty-eight times in Matthew, fourteen times in Mark, and twenty-six times in Luke.

While the first-century Jews were anticipating the appearance of Elijah, the Prophet, and the Christ *(John 1:19–28; 6:14; 7:40)*, they were not expecting the appearance of one known as "the Son of Man." What is the origin of this description, and why did Jesus choose to refer to Himself this way?

The most likely source is Daniel 7:13–14: *"I saw in the night visions, and behold, with the clouds of heaven there came one like a son of man, and he came to the Ancient of Days and was presented before him. ¹⁴And to him was given dominion and glory and a kingdom, that all peoples, nations, and languages should serve him; his dominion is an everlasting dominion, which shall not pass away, and his kingdom one that shall not be destroyed."*

This passage describes a heavenly being who also has the appearance of a human being approaching "the Ancient of Days" and receiving from Him a universal dominion. Along with the kingdom is the honor of being seated at the right hand of "the Ancient of Days." It is certainly a portrayal of the position and work of Jesus.

But if the first-century Jews were familiar with and expecting the appearance of "Elijah," or "the Prophet," or the "Christ," why did Jesus choose this unexpected way to describe Himself? The most likely reason is that these other titles had erroneous concepts attached to them. The title "Christ" or "Messiah" also had political connotations in the minds of the Jews. To gain a hearing and to have more time to teach His message, He chose this less "loaded" way to refer to His person and position.

FOR FURTHER READING: Psalm 8; Hebrews 2.

NOTES

Lesson 15

JESUS IS ... THE TEACHER COME FROM GOD
(JOHN 3:2; 11:28; 20:16)

In John 3:2 Nicodemus admits that not only he but others among the leadership of Israel recognize that Jesus is "a teacher come from God." This is a remarkable admission, considering Nicodemus' position. In this context he is introduced as *"a ruler of the Jews" (John 3:1)*, indicating that he was a member of the Sanhedrin *(see also John 7:45–52)*. In John 3:10, Jesus refers to Nicodemus as *"the teacher of Israel,"* indicating that he had a high position and reputation as an instructor to the people. Nicodemus, however, recognized in Jesus a greater teacher than himself and his associates!

In John 11:28, Martha tells Mary, with reference to Jesus, *"The Teacher is here and is calling for you."* Notice the natural way Martha uses this description of Jesus, knowing that her sister would immediately realize who that Teacher is!

In John 20:16, when Mary Magdalene is confronted by the risen Jesus, she finally recognized his voice when He called her by name. In response, she addressed Him as *"Rabboni,"* which John interprets for us as "Teacher."

These passages show us that among those who heard Him (Nicodemus) and those who were closest to Him (Martha and Mary Magdalene) Jesus was known as "the Teacher." This description places Jesus on a level above all other teachers. In their eyes, He was "the" Teacher, indicating that others who taught did not approach His level of authority *(Matthew 7:28–29)* nor to His level of knowledge of God and of God's ways.

As you read the Gospel of John, observe the number of times Jesus' words confound His listeners *(John 3:1–14; 4:7–30; 5:18–47; 6:25:71; 7:14–51; 8:12–59; 9:35–41; 10:22–39; 12:27–50)*. Yet, His teaching was recognized as having an authority behind it that other teachers did not have. In John 7:32 the rulers sent officers to arrest Jesus. In verse 45 the rulers ask the officers, "Why did you not bring him?" Their response was simply, "No one ever spoke like this man!" These officers spoke more truth than they realized! Truly, no one has ever spoken like Jesus.

One error should be avoided at all costs. Recognition of Jesus as "a great teacher" should never bring Jesus down to the level of other great teachers in history. He is not one great teacher among many, but "the Teacher" without equal! Jesus' methods of teaching (parables, asking questions, etc.) have been recognized as the most effective means of teaching, whether to small or large audiences.

No wonder those who heard Jesus were "astonished," not only at what they heard, but at the One Who taught them! As Nicodemus confessed, "You are a teacher come from God!"

FOR FURTHER READING: Matthew 5:1–7:29; Hebrews 1:1–4; Matthew 13:1–52; Matthew 22:15–46.

NOTES

Lesson 16

JESUS IS ... THE UPLIFTED ONE
(JOHN 3:14; 8:28; 12:32–33; 19:18–30)

Three times in the Gospel of John Jesus uses the expression "lifted up." The first two times *(John 3:14; 8:28)*, there may be some question about what Jesus means by the expression. The third time *(John 12:32–33)*, John explains the meaning of the phrase by saying, *"He said this to show by what kind of death He was going to die."*

The word translated "lifted up" in these contexts in John is translated "exalt" in other contexts *(cf. Matthew 11:23; Luke 1:52; Luke 14:11)*. When Nicodemus heard Jesus use this phrase in John 3:14, it may not have registered that Jesus was speaking of something other than an exalted place of honor and power. The same may have been true of the audience in John 8:28 and in John 12:32. However, Jesus certainly knew that His "lifting up" would not be viewed by the world as a position of honor and power!

In the first text, Jesus likens His lifting up to Moses' setting up a bronze serpent in the middle of the Israelites' camp, so the ones bitten by a deadly snake could look on it and not die *(see Numbers 21:4–9)*. Notice Jesus said, *"And as Moses lifted up the serpent in the wilderness, so **must** the Son of Man be lifted up ..."* (emphasis mine, KWB). The word "must" indicates absolute necessity. Just as the bronze serpent was the only remedy God provided in Numbers 21, so the "lifting up" of Jesus on the cross is the only remedy for sinful mankind today.

In John 8:28 Jesus stated, *"When you have lifted up the Son of Man, then you will know that I am he, and that I do nothing on my own authority, but speak just as the Father taught me."* Jesus indicates that His "lifting up" will be a testimony to the truth of His claims of being the Son. The phrase "I am he" translates a Greek phrase that is sometimes translated simply "I am." That same phrase occurs in John 8:58 where the translators do not add the word "he," and Jesus' opponents readily understood the claim He was making! If we read John 8:28 without the word "he," it reads, *"When you have lifted up the Son of Man, then you will know that I am, and that I do nothing on my own authority, but speak just as the Father taught me."* Jesus is using the expression *"I am"* to claim deity, equality with the Father. Jesus is indicating that the cross would be a witness to His deity. When His words from the cross are read, and when the events surrounding the cross are seen, it should be evident that His claims were indeed attested!

In John 12:32–33 Jesus asserts, *"And I, when I am lifted up from the earth, will draw all people to myself."* Here, Jesus is saying that His "lifting up" would be a means of attracting people from all over the world to Himself. In the context, Greeks were asking if they could see Jesus, apparently for an interview, rather than to catch a glimpse of Him from a distance. Jesus viewed the cross as a magnet, drawing people to Him.

After His death on the cross, Jesus was "lifted up" to glory and power *(Luke 24:50–53; Acts 1:10–11; 2:29–36)*.

FOR FURTHER READING: Exodus 3:13–15; Numbers 21:4–9; 1 John 2:1–2; 4:7–11.

NOTES

Lesson 17

JESUS IS ... THE ONE SENT FROM GOD
(John 3:34; 4:34; 5:30, 37–38; 6:38–39, 44, 57; 7:16, 18, 28–29, 33; 8:16, 18, 26, 29, 42; 9:4; 10:36; 11:42; 12:44–46; 14:24; 15:21; 17:8, 18, 21, 23, 25; 20:21)

From the number of Scriptures listed above, it is obvious that this is the most frequent description of Jesus in the Gospel of John. Jesus was aware of the source of His authority and of His power. From these texts let us learn the following lessons from Jesus:

1) He was sent to speak God's words *(John 3:34; 8:28; 7:16; 14:24)*
2) He was sent to do God's works *(John 5:36; 9:4; 17:4)*
3) He was sent to do the Father's will *(John 4:34; 5:30; 6:38–39)*
4) He was sent to judge righteously and in truth *(John 8:16, 26)*
5) He was sent to please His Father *(John 8:29)*
6) He was sent to reveal the Father Who sent Him *(John 12:45)*
7) He was sent to give life to the world *(John 6:57)*

On the other hand, our responsibility is to:

1) Believe the Father sent Him *(John 5:37, 38; 8:18; 10:36; 11:42; 12:44; 17:8, 25)*
2) Love the One the Father sent *(John 8:42)*
3) To be united under the authority of Christ so the world will know the Father sent Him *(John 17:21, 23)*.

Let this study of Jesus' submission to the One Who sent Him create in your heart a desire to submit to His authority!

FOR FURTHER READING: Hebrews 3:1–6.

NOTES

Lesson 18

JESUS IS ... THE GIVER OF LIVING WATER
(JOHN 4:10–14; 7:37–39)

Water is necessary for life to exist. One can live much longer without food than without water. Dehydration in our bodies can occur gradually and yet produce grave consequences, sometimes requiring hospitalization to restore one to health. Most of us have ready access to water by turning a faucet. In other parts of the world, water is a precious commodity, obtained with great effort by traveling a long distance, perhaps more than once daily.

When Jesus spoke of the "living water" to the Samaritan woman *(John 4:10–14)*, her first thought was about convenience. If she could have access to such a source of water, she would no longer have to come to the well to draw water. Before we judge her too harshly, if we were in her situation, we would likely be attracted to the convenience of not having to make the daily trek to the community well! In fact, even with our conveniences, we still try to find more of them. Unfortunately, Jesus is still simply a convenience to many!

In John 7:37–49, Jesus was attending the Feast of Booths in Jerusalem. This Feast was designed to remind the people of the provision God had made during the wilderness wanderings, recorded in Exodus through Deuteronomy. Part of this festal celebration included drawing water from the Pool of Siloam and pouring it on the base of the altar, specifically reminding the people of God's provision of water from the rock *(cf. Exodus 17:1–7; Numbers 20:2–13)*. In this context, Jesus' claim to provide "living water" would have been especially significant for his audience. John identifies the "living water" as the Spirit who would be given after Jesus' glorification *(cf. Acts 2:15–38)*.

As the Giver of Living Water, Jesus is indispensable for spiritual life. He is not just one of several options for eternal life. He is the only option available for us. He is the only "community well" from which eternal life may be drawn!

FOR FURTHER READING: Leviticus 23:33–43; Psalm 42:1, 2; Isaiah 55:1–5; Zechariah 13:1; Matthew 5:6; 1 Corinthians 10:1–4; Revelation 22:17.

NOTES

Lesson 19
JESUS IS ... THE SAVIOR OF THE WORLD
(JOHN 4:42)

When the word "savior" comes to mind, especially in the context of the New Testament, most probably think of salvation from sin. That concept is present in many passages and must not be minimized. However, the New Testament also uses the words "save, saved, savior" to describe rescue or deliverance from physical disease *(Matthew 9:21)*, or from a natural disaster *(Matthew 8:25)*. Still, the most common use of "save, saved, savior" is with reference to salvation from sin.

In John 4, Jesus traveled from Jerusalem to Galilee, and rather than by-passing Samaria he chose to go through that country. After his conversation with the woman he met when she came to draw water, she went back to the town of Sychar and reported, *"Come, see a man who told me all that I ever did. Can this be the Christ?" (John 4:29)*. The people of Sychar then went out to see this man for themselves. At first, they believed because of the woman's testimony. Later they told her, *"It is no longer because of what you said that we believe, for we have heard for ourselves, and we know that this is indeed the Savior of the world" (John 4:42)*.

At the beginning of this account, we are told that Jews and Samaritans had no dealings with each other *(John 4:9)*. Remember that when Jesus was speaking with the woman, she asked about the proper place of worship, which was a major point of contention between the Jews and Samaritans and dated back to the Assyrian captivity recorded in 2 Kings 17:24–41. When Nehemiah led the project of rebuilding the walls of Jerusalem, he was opposed by the Samaritans, among others *(Nehemiah 4:1–9)*. The division was sealed with the Samaritans' building a temple on Mount Gerizim, and even having their own Scriptures, known as "the Samaritan Pentateuch."

Considering the source of this confession, it is remarkable that these Samaritans would demonstrate such faith. It is important to notice that while the Jews were looking for a "nationalistic Messiah," a Messiah that would restore their kingdom and fortunes, these Samaritans recognized in Jesus the Messiah who would be "the Savior of the world." They had a broader view of the scope of Jesus' mission than did the Jews!

FOR FURTHER READING: Luke 10:25–37; Luke 17:11–19; John 8:48; Acts 8:4–25; 1 John 2:1–2.

NOTES

Lesson 20
JESUS IS ... THE JUDGE
(John 5:19–30; 12:48)

If a survey were conducted asking for a concept associated in the New Testament with Jesus, His role as Judge may be the one least chosen. Most would like to think of Jesus as Savior of the World, or as the Messiah/Christ, or as the Lamb of God. But to acknowledge Jesus as Judge involves recognizing His authority to determine the standard by which we should live, and to hold us accountable to that standard. Most would rather not be constrained by such standards and would rather not think about being judged for their lifestyle.

In John 5, Jesus makes it clear that He is the One Whom the Father has appointed as Judge. Three important points are emphasized in connection with Jesus as Judge.

In John 5:27, Jesus says, *"And he has given him authority to execute judgment, because he is the Son of Man."* Jesus' perfect life as a human qualifies Him to be the perfect Judge. Based on His facing every temptation and never committing a sin, He can perfectly uphold the standard the Father has given. But, because He has walked where we walk, He can be sympathetic and merciful *(cf. Hebrews 4:15–16)*.

In John 5:22–23 Jesus states, *"For the Father judges no one, but has given all judgment to the Son, that all may honor the Son, just as they honor the Father. Whoever does not honor the Son does not honor the Father who sent him."* The honor accorded one who is charged with the responsibility of upholding the standard of justice must be given to Jesus. In fact, Jesus says that anyone who does not render the proper honor to the Son is dishonoring the Father!

Then, in John 5:30, Jesus affirms, *"I can do nothing on my own. As I hear, I judge, and my judgment is just, because I seek not my own will but the will of him who sent me."* His motive for judgment is not for personal vindication or revenge, nor to advance a personal "agenda," but to complete the will of the Father Who sent Him. This assures us of an impartial judgement from an impartial judge!

John 12:48 adds yet another basis for judgment. There Jesus says, *"The one who rejects me and does not receive my words has a judge; the word that I have spoken will judge him on the last day."* When I was in college, I had professors who had differing approaches to the mid-term and final exams. Some would simply say, "Study everything we have covered in class, including lectures, textbook assignments, and outside readings." Others would go through the notes and textbook and tell us what sections to study to prepare for the exam. Jesus is like the second kind of professor—he has told us the precise standard by which we will be judged!

Are you ready to face the Judge?

FOR FURTHER READING: Acts 17:30, 31; 2 Corinthians 5:10

NOTES

Lesson 21

JESUS IS ... THE BREAD OF LIFE
(John 6:35, 41, 48, 51)

John 6:4 sets the time for the events of this chapter near the time of the Passover. This was one of the most festive times of the year for devout Jews, as they would be reading their Scriptures and re-enacting the Exodus (cf. Exodus, chapters 12 and 13). This was a politically volatile time of year. The Jews would be reminded of God's great deliverance in the past from the Egyptian bondage and longing for a similar intervention to liberate them from the hated Romans. Jesus was still in Galilee, and a large crowd had gathered to hear Him. Not willing to send them home hungry, He fed the multitude by dividing a few loaves and fish among the large crowd. Everyone ate and was satisfied, and still there were leftovers! This is a reminder that when God blesses, He does not give us the "bare minimum requirement." Rather, He blesses abundantly!

Jesus sensed that the crowd was about to come and forcefully take Him and proclaim Him as King *(John 6:15)*. Rather than allow that to happen, He sent His disciples away in a boat, dispersed the crowd, and went up on a nearby mountain and prayed. After walking on the water and catching up with the disciples in the boat, He was in the synagogue in Capernaum the next day when many of the people from that crowd found Him. As they began asking Him questions, Jesus went straight to the heart of the matter, using the analogy of bread to explain His own role in God's plan for humanity. Just as the flesh will waste away and die without proper nutrition, so also the spirit will die without feeding on Jesus and receiving nourishment from Him.

In John 6:52–59 Jesus set forth the challenge that one must eat His flesh and drink His blood. Failure to do this would result in eternal death. This was such a "hard saying" that many turned away and no longer followed Him. Jesus even turned to the Twelve and asked if they wanted to go away as well. Peter responded by asking, *"Lord, to whom shall we go? You have the words of eternal life" (John 6:68)*. Peter understood the point Jesus was making. Jesus was claiming to be the only one through Whom we can be eternally blessed! As food is essential to physical life, so Jesus is essential to spiritual life!

FOR FURTHER READING: Exodus 12:1–14:31; John 6:1–71

NOTES

LESSON 22

JESUS IS ... THE HOLY ONE OF GOD
(JOHN 6:69)

After Jesus made the "hard saying" about eating His flesh and drinking His blood, many who had been following Him decided to turn back and follow Him no more *(John 6:52–65)*. When Jesus asked the Twelve if they wanted to leave as well, Peter made a remarkable statement: *"Lord, to whom shall we go? You have the words of eternal life. And we have believed, and have come to know, that you are the Holy One of God" (John 6:68, 69)*.

The prophet Isaiah frequently used the express "The Holy One of Israel" to describe God *(cf. Isaiah 1:4; 5:19, 24; 10:20; 12:6; 17:7; 29:23 [Holy One of Jacob]; 30:11–12, 15, 29; 31:1; 37:23; 41:14, 16, 20; 43:3, 14; 45:11; 47:4; 48:17; 49:7; 54:5; 55:5; 60:9, 14;)*. It is used once in 2 Kings 19:22 in a context where Isaiah is addressing Hezekiah. The expression is used three times in Psalms *(71:22; 78:41; 89:18)*, and twice in Jeremiah *(50:29; 51:5)*. Ezekiel uses the phrase "Holy One in Israel" once *(39:7)*. It has been suggested that the background for Isaiah's use of the phrase is the vision recorded in Isaiah 6, where he saw the throne room of God and the seraphim circling the throne and crying out in such a loud voice that the threshold of the temple shook: *"Holy, Holy, Holy is the LORD God of Hosts" (Isaiah 6:3)*. God is also referred to as *"the Holy One" (Job 6:10; Proverbs 9:10; 30:3; Hosea 11:9, 12; Habakkuk 1:12; 3:3)*. In Psalm 16:10, the phrase *"your Holy One"* is addressed to God and is applied in Acts 2:27 to the resurrection of Jesus from the dead.

While Peter may not have been able to quote all these passages of Scripture at this point in his life (pre-Pentecost), he no doubt would have been familiar with the usage as being especially applied to God. Thus, his use of "the Holy One of God" is informed by this Old Testament usage. There is little doubt that Peter intended this confession to be similar to the one we read on another occasion recorded in Matthew 16:13–20; Mark 8:27–29; and Luke 9:18–20, where he uses the titles "Christ" and "Son of God."

"The Holy One of God" is a recognition of Jesus' unique relationship to both the Father and the world. He is God's special envoy to the world to rescue it from the peril brought about by sin. Being Himself without sin (Hebrews 4:15), He is Holy to the Lord in a sense no one else ever could be. He is thus the only one who can deliver us from sin!

FOR FURTHER READING: Isaiah 6:1–13, and the references from Isaiah listed above.

NOTES

Lesson 23

JESUS IS ... THE ONE WHO SPOKE LIKE NO ONE ELSE
(John 7:46)

There was always controversy surrounding Jesus, especially when He was in Jerusalem. In John 7, He is attending the Feast of Booths. He did not show Himself publicly until the middle of the Feast *(John 7:14)*. The crowd discussed among themselves whether he would come to the Feast and speculated about His identity. Some viewed Him as a good man, while others thought of Him as a deceiver, or even that He had a demon. Some thought He was the Christ, while others believed the Christ would appear without any kind of background. They all agreed that He was speaking words like no one else had ever spoken, even though He was "unlearned," *i.e.*, without special instruction in the Scriptures *(John 7:14–24)*. The people also realized that the religious leaders were seeking to kill Jesus, and yet He spoke publicly and no one arrested Him. Seeing the signs Jesus was doing, many believed in Him *(John 7:25–31)*.

After Jesus taught in the Temple and the people were again talking about Jesus, the Pharisees decided to arrest Him, and sent officers to bring Jesus to their council *(John 7:32)*. However, when the officers returned without bringing Him, the Pharisees asked, *"Why have you not brought Him?"* Their only defense was, *"No one ever spoke like this man!"* (John 7:45, 46).

Truly, the words of Jesus are the greatest words ever spoken. No one ever spoke with the authority of Jesus *(Matthew 7:28, 29)*, with the compassion of Jesus *(Matthew*

9:35–38), with the challenge of Jesus *(Luke 14:25–33)*, or with the grace of Jesus *(Luke 4:22)*. As He said in John 6:63, *"The words that I have spoken to you are spirit and life."* When people heard Jesus speak, rarely were they neutral about Him. They either recognized Him as one who was a great teacher or even the Christ *(John 7:40, 41)*, or they despised Him and His words *(John 7:12)*.

What is your response to Jesus' words? Do you hear them gladly *(Mark 12:37)*, or do you despise them *(John 7:47–49)*? The words of Jesus will never pass away *(Matthew 24:35)*, because they came from His Father in Heaven *(John 8:28)*. His words are the only words that can lead to eternal life *(John 6:68)*, and they are the only words that will judge you at the last day *(John 12:48–50)*.

FOR FURTHER READING: Matthew 5–7, the Sermon on the Mount.

NOTES

Lesson 24
JESUS IS … THE SINLESS ONE
(JOHN 8:46)

In John 8:46 Jesus asks a remarkable question: *"Which of you convicts Me of sin?"* When it is realized that this question was asked, not of His close friends and followers, but of His enemies, and that it was asked in the heat of controversy, then the audacity of the question can be understood. What is even more remarkable is that no one could convict Him of sin! They resorted to name-calling and slander, but there was no charge of real sin!

When one reads the Gospel accounts of the life of Jesus, one remarkable feature is that Jesus lives a life totally unconscious of sin in His life, and there is no barrier between Himself and His Father in heaven. Earlier in John 8:7–9, Jesus challenged the accusers of an adulterous woman, *"Let him who is without sin among you be the first to throw a stone at her."* The result was that they left one at a time, beginning with the oldest among them. When one is honest before God, there is an awareness of sin in one's life!

Consider other characters in the Bible, and their consciousness of sin. In Isaiah 6, the prophet was shown a vision of the very throne room of God, and all His glory and holiness. Isaiah's response was, *"Woe is me…" (Isaiah 6:5)*, a clear recognition of sin in his life. David is described as *"a man after the LORD's own heart" (1 Samuel 13:14)*, yet he freely confessed his sins when confronted by Nathan *(2 Samuel 12:13)*. He even wrote two psalms confessing his sin *(cf. Psalms 32 and 51)*. Peter, upon seeing one of Jesus' miracles, fell before Him and exclaimed, *"Depart from me, for I am a sinful man, O Lord" (Luke 5:8)*. The apostle Paul, in his first letter to Timothy, called himself *"the foremost sinner" (1 Timothy 1:15–16)*. It is characteristic of men, that as they realize the holy nature of God, they are more impressed with their own unworthiness. The song, "Beneath the Cross of Jesus," expresses this consciousness of sin as follows:

> "Upon that cross of Jesus Mine eye at times can see
> The very dying form of One who suffered there for me;
> And from my smitten heart with tears, Two wonders I confess,
> The wonder of his glorious love, and my unworthiness."

Contrast with this the fact that Jesus never confesses sin, never prays for forgiveness, and displays absolutely no feeling of guilt for ever having done anything contrary to the Father's will. This is eloquent testimony that he considered himself sinless! The Bible writers agree with this assessment *(1 Peter 1:18, 19; 2:22; 1 John 1:10; 3:5; 2 Corinthians 5:21; Hebrews 4:15)*. Pilate could find no evil in Jesus *(Mark 15: 14; Matthew 27:24; Luke 23:14, 15; John 18:38)*. One of the thieves crucified with Jesus said to his fellow thief, *"This man has done nothing wrong" (Luke 23:41)*. Even the centurion who was overseeing the crucifixion of Jesus and the two thieves confessed Jesus' innocence *(Luke 23:47; Matthew 27:54)*.

Only a sinless sacrifice could suffice for our atonement before God. Jesus provided precisely what we needed *(1 Peter 1:18, 19)*.

FOR FURTHER READING: John 8:1–59; Luke 5:1–8; Isaiah 6:1–13.

NOTES

Lesson 25
JESUS IS ... THE I AM
(John 8:58)

John 8 records a heated exchange between Jesus and His opponents. They accused Him of being demon-possessed and called Him a "Samaritan," the most demeaning insult they could hurl at him. At the same time, they pressed their claim to descent from Abraham, which in their eyes settled the matter of their righteous standing before God. On the other hand, Jesus states that they are following their true father, the devil, because they were trying to kill Him. As the dispute escalated, Jesus states, "Your father Abraham rejoiced that he would see my day. He saw it and was glad" *(John 8:56)*. The Jews exclaimed, "You are not yet fifty years old, and have you seen Abraham?" Jesus then responded with the astounding statement, "Truly, truly, I say to you, before Abraham was, I am." The next verse states that his adversaries picked up stones to stone Him. They understood the claim Jesus was making, and in their view it was the most serious blasphemy they had ever heard. Jesus had made other statements that angered them *(cf. John 5:10–18)*, and we will see others in our further studies. In this text, Jesus makes an explicit claim that could not—and cannot—be ignored.

When Jesus used the expression "I Am" as a term of self-identification, it brought to the minds of his audience the occasion of the Lord's confrontation with Moses at the burning bush in Exodus 3, 4. When the Lord told Moses to go to Pharaoh and tell him to release the Hebrews, Moses asks, "If I come to the people of Israel and say to them, 'The God of your fathers has sent me to you,' and they ask me, 'What is his name?' what shall I say to them?" [14] God said to

Moses, "I am who I am." And he said, "Say this to the people of Israel: 'I am has sent me to you' " *(Exodus 3:13, 14)*. This was the LORD's self-identification, a revelation of Himself—His name, His nature, His eternity, and His presence. In other words, this is the essence of deity!

Jesus makes a clear claim to deity in John 8:58. We must examine the evidence presented in the Scriptures and determine the validity of that claim. Our eternal destiny depends on our response to Jesus' claims!

FOR FURTHER READING: Exodus 3, 4.

NOTES

Lesson 26

JESUS IS ... THE DOOR OF THE SHEEPFOLD
(JOHN 10:1–10)

In John 9 Jesus healed a man who had been born blind. The way He healed the man, and the fact that it was a Sabbath, drew the anger of the authorities, and the blind man was interrogated regarding his healing. Jesus was once again accused by the Pharisees of leading the people astray because He ignored their traditions surrounding the observance of the Sabbath. John 10 continues the dialogue of the previous chapter.

Jesus observes in John 10:1–6 that people who have evil designs often use deception and stealth to gain access into places they have no right to go. His illustration of the sheepfold would have been readily understood by His audience, and although we are not as familiar with sheep and their care, we can get the point Jesus was making, even though His hearers did not understand at first.

Jesus then makes another of His "I Am" statements: "Truly, truly, I say to you, I am the door of the sheep" *(John 10:7, repeated in verse 9)*. He plainly states that all who preceded Him were thieves and robbers and did not have the best interests of the sheep in mind. They were using the flock for their own advantage.

What can we learn from the illustration of Jesus as the Door? Just as a door represents the point of access to a house, or a room, or a business, with all the privileges that are found within, so Jesus represents the point of access to the blessings God has in store for us. From this text let us learn:

- Jesus is the only way of access to God's blessings (pasture=food) *(John 10:9)*.
- Jesus is the only way of access to God's security and protection *(John 10:1, 8)*.
- Jesus is the only way of living life abundantly *(John 10:10)*.

Our Creator does not intend for us to barely get by in life, nor does He expect us to just be "survivors." He created us to be victorious, "more than conquerors" *(Romans 8:37)*. Jesus came to give us abundant life, but not in the areas of material prosperity and physical health. The Bible emphasizes that when one follows Jesus, we can have abundant forgiveness *(Isaiah 55:6, 7; Luke 24:45–47)*; abundant love *(Philippians 1:9; 1 Thessalonians 3:11, 12)*; abundant faith *(2 Thessalonians 1:3)*; abundant hope *(Romans 15:13)*; abundant good works *(1 Corinthians 15:58; 2 Corinthians 9:8)*; abundant gratitude *(Colossians 2:6, 7)*; abundant comfort *(2 Corinthians 1:5)*; abundant joy *(2 Corinthians 8:2)*; and abundant grace *(Romans 5:15–21)*.

Are you seeking access to God's blessings by some way other than Jesus? Are you enjoying an abundant life, or just "getting by"?

FOR FURTHER READING: Luke 12:13–21

NOTES

Lesson 27

JESUS IS ... THE GOOD SHEPHERD
(John 10:11–30)

This is the second "sheep" illustration Jesus uses in John 10. As the door of the sheepfold, we learned that Jesus is the only access to the Father's blessings, and He is the only One Who can provide the abundant life our Creator desires us to enjoy (John 10:1–10).

Again, the illustration of the Good Shepherd would have been understood by Jesus' audience more fully than by most of us. Shepherds were commonly seen in the surrounding countryside. While they were not always high on the social scale, they provided a necessary service, and those who were responsible shepherds worked diligently for their employer or family, and for the flock that was given to their care.

One of the best-loved Old Testament passages in Psalm 23, where David, writing as a former shepherd, likens God to a shepherd, and claims Him as his own Shepherd. This passage, among others, would have been familiar to Jesus' audience in John 10. But there are other Old Testament Scriptures that refer to shepherds and sheep, some of which are prophetic of Jesus' work among His people. Ezekiel 34:20–24; 37:24–27; Zechariah 11:4–17 and 13:7–9 all find their fulfillment in Jesus' work as the Good Shepherd. The passages from Ezekiel contrast the selfish shepherds, referring to the civil and religious leaders of the nation, with the One Whom the Lord would raise up from David's house to be the true shepherd. The Zechariah passages refer to the "foolish shepherds," who should be caring for the flock, but do not, and even reject the One Who does protect and provide for the sheep. While these passages are not as familiar to us as Psalm 23, they would have been familiar to the religious leaders of Jesus' day, and His statement would have been interpreted in light of their teachings. No wonder we read the reaction John records in John 10:19–21.

As the Good Shepherd, Jesus:

- Gives his **life** for the sheep *(John 10:11, 15, 17, 18)*.
- **Knows** his sheep and **is known** by his sheep *(John 10:14)*.
- Brings his sheep into **one flock** under the one **shepherd** *(John 10:16)*.
- Gives them **eternal life** *(John 10:28)*.

FOR FURTHER READING: Read the passages from Ezekiel and Zechariah listed above; Matthew 9:35–38; Matthew 26:31 (quoted from Zechariah 13:7); Luke 15:4–7; John 1:29, 36; Revelation 5:5, 6; 7:14–17.

NOTES

Lesson 28

JESUS IS ... THE RESURRECTION AND THE LIFE
(JOHN 11:25)

The Gospel of John records only seven "signs," or miracles, Jesus performed during His earthly ministry. John 11 records the last of these signs. The first six are recorded in John 2:1–11; 4:46–54; 5:1–9; 6:1–14; 6:16–21; and 9:1–7. John is the only one to record this sign, possibly because Lazarus was still living when Matthew, Mark, and Luke wrote their accounts. Lazarus' life was in jeopardy due to the chief priests' jealousy *(John 12:9–11)*, but by the time John wrote, Lazarus had probably passed.

This raises the question about the miracles of "resurrection" in the Gospels and Acts. These people—the daughter of Jairus, Matthew 9:18–26; the son of the widow of Nain, Luke 7:11–17; Lazarus in our current text; Dorcas/Tabitha, Acts 9:36–42; and Eutychus, Acts 20:9–12—were raised from the dead to resume their activities until the time they would pass through the transition of death again. The resurrection of Jesus was different, because He was raised from the dead, given a glorious body, ascended into heaven to be reunited with His Father and to sit in the place of honor and authority at the Father's right hand *(Acts 2:32–36; Psalm 110:1)*.

Jesus' display of power over death by raising others from the dead was a foreshadowing of His own resurrection, by which He demonstrated a complete victory over death! His resurrection is the guarantee that we will be raised, never to die again *(1 Corinthians 15:1–58)*. We have the promise that we will be given a glorious body like His glorious resurrection body *(Philippians 3:20, 21; 1 John 3:1–3)*.

When Martha, the sister of Lazarus, went out to meet Jesus, she was distraught by the death of her brother. She and her sister Mary had sent a message to Jesus several days earlier, and He took longer to arrive than they thought it should take. Both sisters said that if He had been there, Lazarus could have been healed before he died *(John 11:21, 32)*. His reply to Martha In John 11:25, *"I am the resurrection and the life,"* is an assurance to her, and to us, that in Jesus eternal life is available, and that our physical death is not the end of our existence!

"I am the resurrection and the life" is a declaration Jesus made before His own death and resurrection. His knowledge of where He had come from and where He was going *(John 17:1–5)* provided the total confidence in the truth of this statement. His resurrection provides us with the total confidence that we can inherit the blessings His never-ending life provides us!

FOR FURTHER READING: John 11:1–44; 1 Corinthians 15:1–58; 1 Thessalonians 4:13–18; Hebrews 2:5–18; 1 John 3:1–3; 5:1–12.

NOTES

Lesson 29

JESUS IS ... THE ONE WHO GLORIFIES THE FATHER
(JOHN 12:23, 28; 13:1; 17:1–5)

In John 12:23 Jesus refers to "the hour," a phrase found several times in the Gospel of John (including "my hour," or "my time," or "his time," cf. *John 2:4; 7:6, 8, 30; 8:20; 13:1*). In the earlier texts the "hour" has not yet come, indicating that Jesus' work was on a determined time schedule. In the current texts, Jesus indicates the time is near, referring to the consummation of His work on earth. He refers to both His own glory and the glory of the Father.

"Glory" brings to our minds a vision of luxurious surroundings, beautiful landscape and architecture, expensive clothing, and the ability to satisfy any desire and whim. This is the picture we are accustomed to seeing in advertising campaigns and in the presentation of the "the good life" in various media.

It comes as a shock to us when we read Jesus' view of glory and how He will glorify the Father. Jesus knew that He would glorify the Father by means of enduring the most shameful, humiliating form of execution known in the ancient world. His cross would be the path to His own glory and the way He would glorify the Father in heaven. His reference in John 12:23–33 to His being "lifted up" is a clear reference to His crucifixion *(see also John 3:14–15; 8:28)*.

We are so far removed from the "scandal of the cross" and the "foolishness" of preaching the cross *(cf. 1 Corinthians 1:23–25)* that it is difficult for us to understand the horror associated with crucifixion in the first century.

Crosses have become ornaments on church buildings, pieces of jewelry displayed proudly and prominently, and even symbols placed on automobile bumpers or windows. The cross has become "respectable" to us due to Jesus' crucifixion. The early Christians had to overcome the stigma associated with crucifixion, and they accomplished it because of Jesus' teaching about His path to glory *(cf. John 17:1–5)*. Just as Jesus taught and demonstrated a different concept of greatness (Matthew 20:20–28), so He also taught and demonstrated a different concept of glory!

How are you seeking to glorify the Father and the Son in your life?

FOR FURTHER READING: Matthew 16:24–27; Luke 24:25–27; 1 Corinthians 6:19–20; 11:23–33; Galatians 6:11–17; 1 Timothy 3:16; Revelation 5:1–14.

NOTES

Lesson 30

JESUS IS ... THE HUMBLE SERVANT
(JOHN 13:1–20)

One of the disciples' frequent discussions among themselves involved the subject of greatness in the Kingdom. Matthew, Mark, and Luke record several occasions of their arguments over positions of authority *(Matthew 18:1–4; Mark 9:34–37; Luke 9:46–48)*. Once the mother of James and John even asked Jesus to grant that her sons might have the positions on His right hand and left hand in the Kingdom *(Matthew 20:20–28)*.

Luke 22:24–30 helps us understand the background of Jesus' actions in John 13:1–20. Luke records that on this very occasion the disciples were once again arguing about who among them is the greatest. On other occasions Jesus taught them precepts. This time He gives a demonstration!

Imagine if you can the embarrassment the disciples must have felt. As they were arguing among themselves, Jesus quietly got up from the table, laid aside His outer garment, took a towel and a basin of water, and began washing the feet of the disciples. Nothing was said until it was Peter's turn to have his feet washed. Peter had the reputation of speaking when no one else had anything to say; sometimes he spoke well *(John 6:68–69)*, sometimes not so well *(Matthew 16:21–23)*. This time Peter said what the others were probably thinking—that they were not worthy for Jesus to wash their feet.

There is a lot of controversy about whether Jesus was instituting an action that should be practiced the same way

He did, or if He were giving an object lesson on servanthood. It seems clear that His intention was to teach the lesson that greatness in His kingdom looks different than greatness in worldly kingdoms. Greatness does not depend on position, power, or prestige, but rather in humility, obedience, and service.

Note that Jesus did not say, *"Since I have washed your feet, you also should wash my feet."* Rather, he said, *"Do you understand what I have done to you? You call me Teacher and Lord, and you are right, for so I am. If I then, your Lord and Teacher, have washed your feet, you also ought to wash **one another's** feet. For I have given you an example, that you also should do just as I have done to you" (John 13:12–15).*

When anyone thinks they are too important to render service, of whatever nature, to another, that person has failed to follow the example Jesus set!

What action do you consider to be beneath you? Whom do you think is not worthy of your service? Aren't you glad Jesus did not think that of us?

FOR FURTHER READING: Matthew 11:28–30; 25:31–46; Mark 9:33–37; Philippians 2:1–11.

NOTES

Lesson 31

JESUS IS ... COMING AGAIN
(JOHN 14:1–4)

During World War II, when General Douglas MacArthur was forced to withdraw American troops from Luzon in the Philippine Islands, he made the statement that has become famous: "I shall return!" He said that to assure the people of Manila that his retreat was temporary and should not be interpreted as deserting them to the hands of the Japanese.

In John 14:3 Jesus makes a similar statement: *"If I go and prepare a place for you, I will come again and will take you to myself, that where I am you may be also."* Jesus is speaking words of comfort and assurance to the disciples.

John 13–16, record Jesus' intimate conversation with his disciples the night before His crucifixion. He knows what is about to take place, and He has tried to prepare the disciples for the crisis they are about to face. He also knows that they still do not understand what He has tried to tell them. Within a few short hours Jesus will be betrayed by Judas, disowned by Peter, forsaken by all of them, sentenced to death by the Jewish Sanhedrin, and crucified by the Romans. The expectations of the disciples will be shaken to the core. So, Jesus assures them that His departure is not the last word.

In the same way, each of us can find comfort and confidence in Jesus' promise to return. Our hearts are filled with troubles from a variety of causes, and if we are focused only on our present circumstances we can be overcome by sorrow and grief. Looking forward to Jesus' coming again is a strong source of encouragement, provided we are prepared for His coming.

The Bible teaches that we do not know the time of His coming and that He may appear at any moment. For some the return of Christ will not be a happy event *(John 5:28–29)*. For others it will be the consummation of a life of devoted service to the Lord of all creation.

The same writer, John, states in Revelation 22:20, *"He who testifies to these things says, 'Surely I am coming soon.' Amen. Come, Lord Jesus!"*

Does the thought of Jesus return fill you with joy or dread? Are you able to say with John, "Amen. Come, Lord Jesus"?

FOR FURTHER READING: Matthew 24:36–25:46; 1 Thessalonians 4:13–5:11.

NOTES

Lesson 32
JESUS IS ... THE WAY
(JOHN 14:6)

In our reading through the Gospel of John, we have read several statements made by Jesus beginning with "I am..." *(John 6:35; 8:12, 58; 9:5; 10:7, 11; 11:25)*. These "I am" statements are unique to the Gospel of John and serve to emphasize aspects of Jesus identity, work, and relationship both to the Father and to humanity.

When Jesus states, *"I am the way,"* He makes a claim that sets Him apart from the founders of the "world religions." Whereas other leaders claimed to be seeking the path of enlightenment or pointing others to the way to peace and life, Jesus goes far beyond by claiming to be the way!

One of the contrasts between the revelation of God in the Bible and the teachings found in other "holy books" is that whereas other religions are the record of men seeking God, the Bible reveals God's seeking man. God initiates the process of reconciling mankind to Himself through Jesus *(cf. 2 Corinthians 5:18–21)*. Many ignore Jesus and instead expend money, time, and energy seeking for the One Who has already made Himself known in the person of Jesus.

After stating *"I am the way,"* Jesus continues by saying, *"No one comes to the Father except through Me."* It is possible to read this quickly and miss the significance of what Jesus is saying. This is an exclusive claim! While some are content to acknowledge Jesus as a great teacher, prophet, or "holy" man, they are not willing to admit that He is the only way of salvation. Jesus does not leave us the option of choosing to follow Him part of the time and mix in the teachings of other religious leaders. If one intends to have eternal fellowship with the Father, it is necessary to go through Jesus, and only through Jesus!

Whom are you following? Do you read your New Testament and take part of it as truth while adding some of the Koran or the Hindu or Buddhist "holy writings"? Do you admit the claim of Jesus that He is the only way to the Father?

FOR FURTHER READING: 2 Corinthians 5:16–21; 1 Peter 3:18–22; 1 John 1:1–10.

NOTES

Lesson 33
JESUS IS ... THE TRUTH
(JOHN 14:6)

Jesus connected *"I am the way"* with *"the truth."* Again, this is an exclusive claim made by Jesus. In the same way that Jesus is the only way to the Father, so He is also the only One Who reveals the truth about the Father and how to live with Him eternally.

"Truth" has become a controversial subject in modern culture. Postmodern philosophy has indoctrinated a large segment of the population with the notion that nothing is absolutely true. "Truth" has become relative rather than objective. "Truth" is a matter of interpretation and each one's "truth" is as viable as another's. It is a moot point for anyone to appeal to an objective standard of true and false, right and wrong, good and evil.

This philosophy shows up in subtle ways in Bible studies. A popular way of conducting a class is to ask each person, "What does this Scripture mean to you?" While personal application of Scripture is necessary, the question implies that Scripture has no meaning in itself. Each one is free to interpret the text in their own way, and no one's interpretation is vested with an authority denied to a different interpretation. The result is an inability to arrive at an objective meaning and application of Scripture. Following this approach to its logical conclusion would result in the same situation as described in Judges 21:25, where "Everyone did what was right in his own eyes."

Jesus' claim, *"I am ... the truth,"* leads to several observations.

First, there is "truth." Truth exists and is real. Truth is objective, not relative. Jesus' use of the definite article, *"**the** truth,"* indicates that competing perspectives are not true.

Second, truth can be known. Contrary to popular thinking, it is possible to come to a knowledge of the truth and know that it is true.

Third, Jesus did not just teach truth, He embodied truth. Every word He spoke, every act He did, was true. Everything about Jesus was in perfect accordance with the Father's will, which is the ultimate truth.

Fourth, in the same way that Jesus is the only way to the Father, so His teaching and example is the only body of teaching and pattern of living that will bring us to the Father's presence.

Whose "truth" are you following? Have you bought into the modern philosophy that nothing is true except what you think is true? Are you willing to learn the truth by studying seriously the life and words of Jesus?

FOR FURTHER READING: John 8:31–32; John 17:17; Colossians 1:3–8; 1 John 2:21–25; 2 John 1–13; 3 John 1–8.

NOTES

Lesson 34

JESUS IS ... THE ONE WHO SENDS THE HELPER
(JOHN 14:16–18, 26; 15:26–27; 16:7–15)

In John 14, 15 and 16 Jesus used a word four times to describe the Holy Spirit and His work with the apostles. The word is translated *"Helper"* in the ESV, and others. The Greek word is *"paracletos"* and refers to *"one called alongside to render aid, comfort, support."* By studying these passages carefully, we can learn great lessons about the work of the Spirit in the ministry of the apostles.

A careful examination of the context of these chapters indicates that Jesus is speaking to the Twelve, minus Judas *(cf. John 13:21–30)*. The promises Jesus makes concerning the Spirit and what He would do for the apostles should not be applied indiscriminately to all Christians. The fulfillment of these promises began at the Feast of Pentecost recorded in Acts 2 *(cf. Acts 1:4–8; 2:1–36)*. The apostles were still lacking in understanding Jesus' teaching and what He was expecting from them. He knew that His arrest, trial, and crucifixion would devastate them. He gives them these promises to provide assurance and comfort to help them get through the time between His crucifixion and resurrection.

The work of the Helper—who is described as "the Spirit of truth"—included the following aspects:

1) He would ***comfort*** the apostles by His presence *(John 14:16–18)*.
2) He would ***remind*** the apostles of Jesus' words *(John 14:25–26)*.

3) He would **testify** concerning Jesus *(John 15:26–27)*.
4) He would **convict** the world and **guide** the apostles into all truth *(John 16:5–15)*.

The book of Acts records the work of the Spirit through the words and works of the apostles. This is the fulfillment of Jesus' promises in these chapters. Our responsibility is to listen to the instruction of the Spirit as revealed through the words these men spoke and wrote in the New Testament.

Since the Spirit is called "the Spirit of truth" in John 16:13, all that He reveals is consistent with the will of both the Father and the Son. Anyone who claims to receive a revelation from the Spirit that contradicts the doctrine of the New Testament is either deceived or a deceiver *(cf. Galatians 1:6–9; 1 John 4:1–4)*. On the other hand, if one is led by the Spirit, he is following the teaching of the Spirit as revealed in the New Testament.

In John 14:16 Jesus said, "I will send you another Helper," referring to the Spirit. In 1 John 2:1 the word *"paracletos"* is used to refer to Jesus, our "advocate with the Father." Thus, Jesus is the first Helper, and the Spirit is "another" Helper.

To whom are you listening? What Spirit are you following?

FOR FURTHER READING: 1 John 2:1–2; 4:1–4.

NOTES

Lesson 35
JESUS IS ... THE TRUE VINE
(JOHN 15:1–11)

The last *"I am"* statement in the Gospel of John is *"I am the true vine" (John 15:1)*. This figure would have been especially significant to Jesus' disciples and to John's first readers. The **vine** was—and is—prevalent throughout Palestine, and was frequently used in the Old Testament as a symbol for Israel *(cf. Isaiah 5:1–7; Jeremiah 2:21–22; Ezekiel 15:1–8; 17:1–10; 19:10–14; Hosea 10:1–2; Psalm 80:8–16)*. Several of Jesus' parables feature a vineyard and husbandmen: The Parable of the Laborers in the Vineyard *(Matthew 20:1–16)*; The Parable of the Two Sons *(Matthew 21:28–32)*; The Parable of the Wicked Tenants *(Matthew 21:33–44)*.

Jesus teaches the following lessons with this illustration:

1) His use of the word "abide," repeated ten times in John 15:4–11, teaches the lesson of persistence and consistency in living. This word is sometimes translated "remain," "live," "dwell," or "continue," suggesting habitual conduct.

2) The vine is the source of life and supports the branches. A branch separated from the vine is not only fruitless, but dying or dead. As a Christian, we can do nothing profitable without Christ *(John 15:4–5)*. Contrast that with Paul's confidence in Philippians 4:13—*"I can do all things through him who strengthens me."*

3) The Father, as the vinedresser, prunes the fruitful branches to make them more fruitful *(John 15:1–2)*. Pruning may not be pleasant, but the intention is to strengthen the branch so it can produce more fruit.

A Christian facing a "pruning" season has a reason to rejoice rather than give up.
4) Bearing fruit is the way a Christian glorifies God *(John 15:8)*. This is one of the primary expectations of a Christian. Fruit-bearing includes teaching and converting others and bringing forth the "fruit of the Spirit" in one's attitudes and conduct *(Galatians 5:22–23)*.
5) Abiding in Jesus includes abiding in His word, His love, and keeping His commandments *(John 15:7, 9–10)*. Love and obedience are two sides of the same coin.
6) All that Jesus teaches in this paragraph has joy as the goal *(John 15:11)*. Although it is a common perception that the Christian life is a drudgery—and that may be the fault of Christians who demonstrate little or no joy in their lives—Jesus intends for His people to be filled with joy!

Are you a fruit-bearing branch? Are you practicing both love and obedience? How full is your joy?

FOR FURTHER READING: Read the Old Testament references and the parables referred to above.

NOTES

LESSON 36

JESUS IS ... THE ONE WHO LAYS DOWN HIS LIFE FOR HIS FRIENDS
(JOHN 15:13–14)

Already in the Gospel of John Jesus has referred to His death *(John 3:14–16; 7:19, 33–34; 8:28; 10:17–18; 12:23–24, 32–33)*. In this conversation with His disciples, Jesus speaks more clearly about His death. In fact, Jesus was crucified and buried within 24 hours.

When reading about the death of Jesus, it is difficult for us to approach the subject with a fresh perspective. Most of us have heard sermons, participated in Bible classes, and read widely, about the death of Jesus. That is good, because the death of Jesus stands at the center of God's purpose in redeeming mankind. But we run the risk of reading too quickly through the statements of Jesus regarding His death.

Notice that Jesus begins this statement with a comparison, *"Greater love has no one than this ..."*. The implication is that the love Jesus is about to describe is the greatest love known to humans!

The greatest love is to *"lay down one's life"* on behalf of others. *"Laying down"* indicates a voluntary action *(cf. John 10:17–18)*. Jesus' death was not simply a result of His making powerful enemies who were able to orchestrate His death. He did not go to the cross kicking and screaming, struggling to escape the Sanhedrin or the Romans. Instead, He prayed for the strength to face the horror of bearing the sin of the world, and *"gave Himself for our sins" (1 Corinthians 15:1–4)*. His death was both voluntary and intentional.

Jesus specifies those who will benefit from His death. He lays down His life *"for his friends."* This word is a beautiful word in any language. Jesus was criticized for being *"a friend of tax-collectors and sinners" (Matthew 11:19; Luke 15:1–2)*. His eating with people considered as outcasts scandalized the Pharisees and lawyers. It went far beyond their limits of friendship.

While Jesus' death is sufficient to save "the whole world" *(1 John 2:1–2)*, those who will benefit from it—His friends—are those who "do what I command you." As in John 15:10, so here Jesus emphasizes the requirement of obedience to Him and His words. That is His definition of friendship.

Are you a friend of Jesus? Do you pass the requirement of obedience?

FOR FURTHER READING: John 14:15–24; 1 John 5:1–5.

NOTES

Lesson 37

JESUS IS ... THE GREATEST EXAMPLE OF LOVE
(JOHN 15:12)

"**J**esus loves me, this I know, for the Bible tells me so." Can you read that line without having a tune in your mind? This "children's song" states one of the most profound theological themes revealed in Scripture.

"Love" is a difficult word to define. "Love" can describe one's reaction to pizza, football, a movie, a book, or a person. It is frequently used as a euphemism for sexual gratification. It is also one of the most frequently used words in the Bible.

The Greek language is more nuanced regarding love, having four different words translated by our one English word. The word referring to sexual love is not found in the Bible. The word for natural human affection is found twice in the New Testament in the negative form and is translated "heartless" in the ESV *(Romans 1:31; 2 Timothy 3:3)*. It signifies "lack of natural affection." The other two words are found frequently in the New Testament. One refers to the warm affection between friends. The other refers to the choice to love someone regardless of whether there is anything loveable about the object of the one loved, or if the love is returned.

In the Gospel of John, the word for "friendship love" is found 13 times in 10 verses *(cf. John 5:20; 11:3, 36; 12:25; 15:19; 16:27; 20:2; 21:15–17)*. The word for "choosing love" is found 37 times in 27 verses *(cf. John 3:16, 19, 35; 8:42; 10:17; 11:5; 12:43; 13:1, 23, 34; 14:15, 21, 14:23–24, 14:28, 14:31; 15:9, 12, 17; 17:23–24, 26; 19:26; 21:7, 15–16, 20)*.

As we look more carefully at these passages, we find that God chose to love us and to send His Son to save us (John 3:16). In a negative sense, John 12:43 states, *"Nevertheless, many even of the authorities believed in him, but for fear of the Pharisees they did not confess it, so that they would not be put out of the synagogue; for they loved the glory that comes from man more than the glory that comes from God."* In both cases a choice was made: God chose to love us in spite of ourselves; the authorities chose the glory that comes from man above the glory that comes from God.

With that in mind, John 15:12 uses the word that indicates choice. Jesus demonstrates the love of choosing to lay down His life rather than trying to find an easier, more convenient way. That is why His death is the greatest demonstration of love.

What choices are you making? Have you considered that your choices reflect your "true love"?

FOR FURTHER READING: In addition to the verses from the Gospel of John listed above, read Romans 5:6–8; 8:31–39; Galatians 2:20–21; 1 John 4:7–12.

NOTES

Lesson 38

JESUS IS ... THE ONE WHO OVERCOMES THE WORLD
(JOHN 16:33)

These are the last words Jesus spoke to the disciples before his arrest and crucifixion. They are words of comfort, encouragement, and confidence. They are remarkable when the circumstances are fully considered. The men who first heard these words would see Jesus bound, tried, convicted, beaten, and crucified within a few hours. How could Jesus possibly claim to have overcome the world?

Jesus overcame, or conquered, the world in the following ways:

1) He had overcome the **temptation** of the world *(cf. Matthew 4:1–11).*
2) He had overcome the **cares** of the world *(cf. Matthew 13:22).*
3) He had overcome the **schemes** of the world *(cf. Acts 4:23–28).*
4) He had overcome the **ruler** of the world *(cf. John 12:30–32; Ephesians 2:1–3; 2 Corinthians 4:3–4).*
5) Within a short time after saying these words, Jesus would overcome death itself *(John 20–21).*

Jesus' victory paves the way for us to share in that victory. He is our "forerunner"—or pioneer, trailblazer—going before us to prepare the way *(John 14:1–3; Hebrews 6:13–20)*. Note these passages:

1 Corinthians 15:57—*"But thanks be to God, who gives us the victory through our Lord Jesus Christ."*

1 John 5:4–5—*"For everyone who has been born of God overcomes the world. And this is the victory that has overcome the world—our faith. Who is it that overcomes the world except the one who believes that Jesus is the Son of God?"*

Revelation 12:11—*"And they have conquered him by the blood of the Lamb and by the word of their testimony, for they loved not their lives even unto death."*

Do you want to be a winner? Are you trying to win by yourself, or are you striving to share the victory Jesus has won?

FOR FURTHER READING: Romans 8:31–39; Revelation 2:1–3:22. Observe that the letters to the seven churches include a promise to "the one who overcomes," anticipating Revelation 12:11!

NOTES

Lesson 39

JESUS IS ... THE ONE WHO DRINKS THE CUP
(JOHN 18:11)

In this verse Jesus makes a cryptic reference to a "cup" He must drink. That cup was given to Him by the Father. To what is Jesus referring? What is this cup, and why did the Father give it to Jesus to drink?

In another context, recorded in Matthew 20:20–28 and Mark 10:35–45, Jesus refers to "drinking the cup." The context indicates that the cup would be a cup of suffering. James and John have just asked Jesus to grant them the places of highest honor in His kingdom, and Jesus challenges them by asking, *"Are you able to drink the cup that I drink, or to be baptized with the baptism with which I am baptized?" (Mark 10:38)*. After assuring Jesus they were able, Jesus affirmed that they would indeed drink the cup and endure His baptism. Suffering appears to be the meaning of both the cup and baptism in this context.

In the background of these references in the New Testament are several Old Testament passages. Isaiah 51:17, 22; Jeremiah 25:15–28; and Ezekiel 23:28–35. Isaiah and Ezekiel both refer the "cup" of God's wrath as poured and ready for Judah and Jerusalem to drink. Jeremiah places the "cup" in the hands of all the surrounding nations upon whom the armies of Nebuchadnezzar are about to come, and afterwards Babylon will also drink from that cup. The cup in all of these passages is described as "wrath," "horror and desolation," "sword and famine," "staggering." They serve as warnings to those nations, including Judah, that God's wrath will be felt through the instrument of Babylon.

When Jesus, the night before His crucifixion, refers to drinking the cup His Father has given Him, He is referring to God's wrath against sin. Just as the sinfulness of Judah and the surrounding nations brought God's wrath in punishment, so our sins place us under the wrath of God *(Romans 1:18–3:20)*.

Sin must be punished, but God loves us so much He does not want us to suffer the eternal consequences for our sins. The word "propitiation" is used in Romans 3:21–26; Hebrews 2:17; and in 1 John 2:2; 4:10. This word means *"appeasement necessitated by sin"* (*BDAG* Lexicon, 473–473), and refers to the sacrifice that makes that appeasement possible.

When Jesus died on the cross, He suffered more than the physical agony shared by the two thieves who were crucified on each side of him. He suffered the wrath of God against sin! This helps us understand the cry of Jesus, *"My God, my God! Why have you forsaken Me?" (Matthew 27:46)*. It was the "cup of God's wrath" against sin Jesus was drinking.

What effect does Jesus' willingness to "drink the cup" have on your life? How can you show your gratitude for His drinking the cup?

FOR FURTHER READING: 2 Corinthians 5:16–21.

NOTES

Lesson 40

JESUS IS ... THE OBEDIENT ONE
(JOHN 17:4; 19:30)

John 17 has been called "Jesus' High Priestly Prayer," and more popularly, "The (Real) Lord's Prayer." John has recorded for us Jesus' intercessory prayer, and it can be divided into three parts: Jesus Prays for Himself *(John 17:1–5)*; Jesus Prays for His Disciples *(John 17:6–19)*; and Jesus Prays for Us *(John 17:20–26)*.

In John 17:4 Jesus states, *"I glorified you on earth, having accomplished the work that you gave me to do."* Jesus is saying that everything the Father had planned and purposed, He had brought to its appointed conclusion.

Then, in John 19:30, in what may have been His dying breath, Jesus said, *"It is finished."* This English phrase translates a single Greek word. A literal translation may be, "Finished!" In my own reading of this passage, I can hear Jesus shout this as a cry of victory, rather than a sigh of resignation. He realized that everything He could do and had been sent to do had been done. Now it was left to the Father to raise Him from the dead.

Consider the following seven areas that were brought to their completion:

1) The Life of *Suffering* He Endured Was Finished *(Isaiah 53:3; Matthew 16:21)*
2) The Life of *Example* He Lived Was Finished *(1 Peter 2:18–24; John 13:15).*
3) The *Prophecies* He Fulfilled Were Finished *(Isaiah 7:14; 9:6–7; 52:13–53:12; Luke 24:25–27, 44–47)*

4) The *Law* He Came to *Fulfill* Was Finished! *(Matthew 5:17; Colossians 2:13–14; Ephesians 2:14–17; Romans 10:4).*
5) The *Will* of God He Came to *Obey* Was Finished! *(John 5:30; Philippians 2:5–8; Hebrews 10:8–10).*
6) The "Scheme of Redemption" for which He Shed His Blood Was Finished! *(Ephesians 1:7; 1 Peter 1:17–19; Matthew 20:26–28; 26:27–28; Revelation 1:4–6; 5:9–10; 7:13–14).*
7) His Separation from the Father Was Finished! *(John 17:5; Matthew 27:46; John 20:17).*

From Jesus we learn that obedience is not convenient. His obedience to the Father's will extended *"even to the death of the cross"* (Philippians 2:8).

How far are you willing to go in your obedience to the Father's will? Are you obedient only as long as it's convenient?

FOR FURTHER READING: Hebrews 5:7–9; Revelation 5:1–14.

NOTES

Lesson 41

JESUS IS ... LORD AND GOD
(JOHN 20:28)

Thomas is known to most readers of the Bible as "doubting Thomas." When the disciples were together in the evening of the day Jesus was raised from the dead, "Thomas was not with them" *(John 20:24)*. When they told him they had seen Him alive, Thomas did not believe them, and strongly stated, "Unless I see in his hands the mark of the nails, and place my finger into the mark of the nails, and place my hand into his side, I will never believe" *(John 20:25)*.

A week later Jesus appeared again, and this time Thomas was with them. Jesus' first order of business was to address Thomas and offer His hands, feet, and side as the evidence Thomas had requested. Whether Thomas put his fingers in the nail scars and his hand in Jesus' side is not stated. The text indicates that was unnecessary. What we are told is that Thomas made a remarkable confession: "My Lord and my God" *(John 20:28)*.

Those words sound blasphemous. Were it not for all that John has recorded up to this time, they would sound scandalous. They jolt us the same way some of Jesus' claims jolted His audiences earlier in the Gospel *(cf. John 5:18)*.

Jesus commends Thomas for his confession of faith, but gently chastises him for his previous doubts *(John 20:29)*. At the same time, Jesus pronounces a blessing on those who do not require physical evidence to believe. That includes those who would believe the testimony of the eyewitnesses who preached the resurrection and those who would believe the written record of their testimony.

The confession *"Lord and God"* is reminiscent of Old Testament language. Thomas made a confession that would have been difficult for Jews who took seriously the teaching that there is one God *(cf. Deuteronomy 6:4–6)*. Elevating Jesus to that status marked a distinct recognition of His unique nature. Thomas' use of the personal possessive pronoun "my" demonstrates his understanding that believing in Jesus is personal. Regardless of whether anyone else believed in Jesus or not, Thomas believed.

The same is true today. We must disregard the numbers and reputation of those who do and do not believe in Jesus. We must make our own decision about Jesus.

Is Jesus your Lord and God? Do you submit to His authority and love Him exclusively?

FOR FURTHER READING: Titus 2:11–14; 2 Peter 1:1–2; Revelation 4:1–5:14.

NOTES

LESSON 42

JESUS IS ... ALIVE
(JOHN 20:1–21:25)

The biographies of famous people usually record facts about the date, place and circumstances of the subject's birth, anecdotes about early life and education, an account of notable accomplishments, and the date and circumstances of their death. There may be an "Epilogue" summarizing the legacy of the person's life and achievements.

Matthew, Mark, Luke, and John record the life of Jesus. John tells us that only a small portion of the signs Jesus performed were recorded *(John 20:30–31; 21:25)*. Only Matthew and Luke record anything about His birth. But all four Gospels devote a large proportion of their records to the death and resurrection of Jesus. What is considered the "Epilogue" of other people's lives is the focal point of these records about Jesus!

The resurrection of Jesus is connected to every significant doctrine in the New Testament:

1) The deity of Jesus *(Romans 1:4)*
2) Baptism *(Colossians 2:12; Romans 6:4; 1 Peter 3:21–22)*
3) The resurrection of all men *(1 Corinthians 15:12–14, 20, 23; Colossians 1:18)*
4) The establishment of the church *(Matthew 16:18; compare Daniel 7:13–14)*
5) The forgiveness of sins *(1 Corinthians 15:16–17; Luke 24:46–47)*
6) The judgment of all men *(Acts 17:30–31)*

7) Salvation *(Romans 10:9–10; 4:25; 5:10; Hebrews 7:25)*
8) Description of God *(Exodus 20:1–2; Jeremiah 16:14–15; Galatians 1:1)*

The resurrection of Jesus was different from other accounts of people who were brought back to life in the New Testament: the daughter of Jairus *(Mark 5:21–24, 35–43)*; the son of the widow of Nain *(Luke 7:11–17)*; and Lazarus *(John 11)*. These all were brought back to life for a while and died again. Jesus was raised never to die again. He was raised to a life that "continues forever" *(Hebrews 7:23–28)*.

Among the most convincing evidences for the resurrection of Jesus is the preaching of the apostles in Acts 2. Less than two months after Jesus' death and resurrection, in Jerusalem where it occurred, Peter and the others proclaimed Jesus as alive from the dead, and no one was able to prove them wrong! Those who were responsible for Jesus' death did not contradict the apostles, nor did they produce His dead body. The apostles continued preaching the resurrection, enduring persecution and even death. Neither did they profit financially from their preaching.

Jesus is alive! Jesus is reigning in heaven! Jesus will come again!

Have you seriously investigated the evidence for Jesus' resurrection? Are you fully convinced that Jesus was raised from the dead and lives today?

FOR FURTHER READING: 1 Corinthians 15:1–58; Philippians 3:20–21; 1 John 3:1–3.

NOTES

CPSIA information can be obtained
at www.ICGtesting.com
Printed in the USA
BVHW061658200421
605394BV00011B/2218